Anger: Our Master or Our Servant

Workbook

By Larry Heath

Communications should be addressed to:
Turning Point Ministries, Inc.
P. O. Box 22127
Chattanooga, TN 37422-2127

Cover Photo: Larry Foster
Cover Design: Graphic Advertising
Layout: Louise Lee

ISBN 1-58119-013-1

Turning Point®

About the Author

Larry Heath serves as Minister of Pastoral Counseling and Marriage Enrichment at First Assembly of God, Concord, North Carolina.

He graduated from Wake Forest University (1962) and holds a Master of Religious Education degree from Southwestern Baptist Theological Seminary (1964), Fort Worth, Texas.

Larry has conducted numerous marriage and family retreats, workshops, and seminars.

Anger: Our Master or Our Servant

Contents

	Page
Introduction	3
Session One — You're Angry! No, I'm Not!	4
Session Two — What Is Anger? Its Composition	11
Session Three — Anger: What Causes It?	16
Session Four — When Anger Is a Sin (Part I)	21
Session Five — When Anger Is a Sin (Part II)	28
Session Six — Beginning Steps in Managing Your Anger	32
Session Seven — Managing Your Anger	36
Session Eight — Managing Anger in Your Marriage and/or Family Relationships	42
Session Nine — Accepting Responsibility for Managing My Anger	49
Selected Bibliography	55

Workbook: *Anger: Our Master or Our Servant*, Turning Point, P. O. Box 22127, Chattanooga, TN 37422-2127

Introduction

Anger: Our Master or Our Servant

The importance of a vibrant, healthy faith is often seen as unrelated to one's feelings. However, it is clear that our growth in our spiritual life is vitally related to our understanding of the role of our emotions and their powerful influence in developing a healthy faith.

The stewardship of our mental health is vital in developing a well-balanced faith. Therefore, it is becoming more and more evident that we see how our feelings function and how biblically to manage or express them.

One of the greatest concerns we have seen in this area is that Christians find it particularly difficult to accept the fact of anger in their lives. Many see anger as a feeling that is contradictory to their faith and "walk in the Spirit."

The Bible presents some clear principles on how to manage anger. This material provides a challenging journey into the powerful emotion of **Anger**.

Few of us have been taught how to live with our feelings. We are taught how to think, but feelings often overwhelm and master the Christian.

With spousal abuse, child abuse, violence, depression, and other problems on the rise in our culture, it is clear that anger and its potential for evil or righteousness need to be addressed from a biblical perspective.

So let's get started on a journey that will hopefully provide new and exciting ways to understand and direct your anger to God's purpose and plan for your life—a healthy Christian life.

> *This material provides a challenging journey into the powerful emotion of* **Anger**.

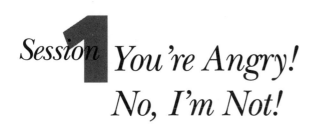

Session **1** *You're Angry!*
No, I'm Not!

Welcome

Welcome to this important journey of growth in your spiritual life. When you think of anger, you may see such an emotion as unrelated to your spiritual growth. How is it that your spiritual and emotional life can be related? Good stewardship of your mental and emotional health is vital to a well-balanced spiritual life. As you begin this study on anger, ask God to help you see it through so that with your commitment and hard work, coupled with God's Word and His blessing, anger will become your servant rather than your master. Spend 30 minutes each day in meditation and prayer. Ask God to help you cooperate with Him to make this journey a successful one.

Self-Awareness

People often struggle with a variety of problems that seem to surface such as marital conflicts, parenting issues, interpersonal and relational difficulties, depression, grief, even physical illness or pain; yet even while these issues are being discussed and addressed, anger often makes its appearance—in overt or covert ways. Often people will not recognize anger as a problem or issue but will deny or hide it.

Anger is a part of being human. All of us have lost our tempers and lashed out at God, ourselves, or others. Many of us have silently boiled in rage or frustration at someone or something.

Perhaps you are reluctant to come to terms with the fact that we are people who get angry. Anger is not a passing fad or "psychological issue" that demands our brief attention. Anger is here to stay. It has been here since creation. We can observe anger in daily life. Most of us don't want to be examples of losing our temper but generally want to appear as controlled, calm, and peaceful.

Anger may be the most common emotional feeling we humans share. It is one of the earliest emotions expressed by an infant.

As the infant develops some security with parents, he will begin to display infant anger and rage. We have all seen that sweet little baby stiffen his body, exhibit a change in facial expressions, scream, and express his frustrations. This is normal in a loving environment where a child expresses anger within certain supportive boundaries set by parents.

Perhaps you have heard the following story:

A mother heard her four-year-old son screaming and crying from the basement where he was watching his father build cabinets. Fearing the boy had been seriously hurt, she opened the door and saw him crying on the steps. "What in the world is wrong with you?" she demanded. Through his tears, the little boy replied, "Daddy hit his thumb with the hammer."

"If daddy hit his thumb with the hammer, then why are you crying?" "Well...I didn't cry at first," he explained, "I laughed."

Children raised in this kind of environment soon learn to hide their anger as much as possible. Children get very little positive help in learning how to manage their angry feelings. Parents need to be thoughtful enough to explain ways in which their child's anger can be expressed with their permission. Children learn to feel guilty for *experiencing* the feelings of anger and down right sinful for *expressing* it.

Read the following 1974 report from the Joint Commission on Mental Health of Children (Dobbins, 78-79).

> *The role of violence and its encouragement in young children must be faced squarely. Some children meet abuse and angry outbursts at the hand of their parents. Nearly all children are exposed to graphic violence over the television screen. Through possible imitation of and identification with these models, patterns of violent behavior may be easily acquired.*
>
> *Of at least equal importance are the patterns by which the young child is taught to handle his own frustrations, his own angry feelings, and the constructive or destructive acts for which he comes to feel responsible. Possibly no other area represents as profound a source of pathology in our culture as the handling of anger and aggression.*

Describe your reaction to this report.

Do children raised in Christian families experience less family violence than secular families?

How good a job are Christian families doing in providing instruction and guidance in the matter of helping family members understand, control, and direct feelings of anger properly?

Workbook: *Anger: Our Master or Our Servant*, Turning Point, P. O. Box 22127, Chattanooga, TN 37422-2127

What are some examples of situations that cause people to respond with anger?

As you can see, your examples of anger in daily life show us that anger can range from irritation to explosive responses in people. The clichés we use to show anger can reveal some interesting information about anger.

What are some common ways we define anger in clichés?

Describe ways we encourage others to control their anger.

What metaphors do we often use?

Without emotional expression, life would be *unfelt* and appear as only rational or cognitive. However, thoughts and behaviors are connected to our feelings. Rational thought alone will not provide the energy needed to function as human beings in experiencing life. We all require feelings to motivate us sufficiently to do the enjoyable in life as well as experience suffering and pain.

How do children, youth, and adults differ in their expression of anger? Give examples.

List below some situations that are examples of anger in various developmental stages of life(childhood, adolescence, adulthood). These may come from personal or other sources.

To better understand ourselves and the emotion of anger, let's examine God's Word on this subject.

Spiritual-Awareness

Read the following scriptures and reflect on what God's viewpoint is regarding anger.

❑ Genesis 1:28

❑ Psalm 7:11

❑ Ephesians 4:26

❑ Ephesians 4:27

❑ Hebrews 12:15

❑ Genesis 4:1-8

Workbook: *Anger: Our Master or Our Servant,* Turning Point, P. O. Box 22127, Chattanooga, TN 37422-2127

Read Mark 3:1-6. Ask yourself these questions:

Did Jesus experience anger?

Describe the place anger played in this event in Jesus's life. Did Jesus sin when He was angry?

Anger is a normal emotion that can be used for good or evil. What have you been taught about expressing anger that is not healthy?

What have you discovered about anger in this session that will help you accept anger as a normal, God-given emotion?

How aware are you of anger in your life and what are some areas in which you may need to make changes?

The Bible encourages us to find ways to manage our anger. As we accept anger as a common part of life, it is imperative that we learn scriptural, practical, and healthy ways to make anger our servant. As you conclude this session and continue your journey into understanding this powerful force, pray for God's guidance to discover where you are in accepting your anger and the need to make it your servant for God's glory.

Study carefully the *Anger Log* and *Anger Expressions* forms on pages 9 and 10. You will see these charts again in Session 7 for later comparisons.

MY ANGER LOG									
Day	1	2	3	4	5	6	7	8	9
Frequency How many times do you get angry each day inwardly or outwardly? Place a number for each day.									
Intensity On the average, from 1-10 what is the intensity of your anger today? (10 = intense; 1= barely breathing)									
Duration How many minutes do you usually remain angry? Use an average.									
Negative Expression How many times does your anger lead to negative expression?									
Positive Expression How many times does your anger lead to positive expression?									
Disturbs Relationships On the average, did your anger today help or hinder relationships? (9= helpful; 1 =disaster)									

Workbook: *Anger: Our Master or Our Servant*, Turning Point, P. O. Box 22127, Chattanooga, TN 37422-2127

Fill out the Anger Expressions chart. Consider the last two times you got angry at each person and how you expressed it. Now observe how you express your anger the next time you get angry at each person.

ANGER EXPRESSIONS

✍ **Mark with a check (✓) how you expressed anger to each person most recently.**

Person	Hold it back	Indirect	Direct
Spouse	_____	_____	_____
Children	_____	_____	_____
Parents	_____	_____	_____
Employer	_____	_____	_____
Coworker	_____	_____	_____
Friends	_____	_____	_____

Which type of expression do you tend to use most?

What can you do to make your anger expression healthier and more productive?

✍ **Think about the following people toward whom you might express anger. How do they respond when you express anger? Write down how you will respond the next time.**

Person	Response	How I will respond differently the next time
Spouse	_____	_____
Children	_____	_____
Mother	_____	_____
Father	_____	_____
Boss	_____	_____
Friends	_____	_____

✍ **Think of a constant provoking behavior or situation and then think of a change that you can make when all else fails.**

Charts taken from *When Anger Hits Home* by Gary Jackson Oliver and H. Norman Wright. 1992. Moody Press. Used by permission.

Session 2

What Is Anger?
Its Composition

Meet with God

Personal Notes

As you begin this study on anger, it is important that you pre-pare your heart for God to condition your mind and heart for any changes that may be needed as you progress through this study. Openness, teachability, and humility are qualities that we all need to develop so that growth and change can be experienced in our lives.

Spend 30 minutes each day in meditation and prayer. Study Psalm 39:1-13; 51:6; 139:23-24. All of these scriptures deal with knowledge of the truth and self-understanding. Ask God to help you position yourself to let Him teach you about anger in your life.

Self-Awareness

We humans often see anger in an exaggerated way. Sometimes simple irritation may be misunderstood as full-blown anger causing us subsequent guilt or fear of this normal human emotion. Anger is a common, human,everyday emotional reaction that people feel in response to a variety of situations.

It begins in infancy, and evidently we don't feel guilty about it. However, as we mature, we do develop guilt about our anger due to our parents' angry responses to us and seeing them get angry with us. In being reared and rearing our children, we all have become very familiar with anger and what it produces.

We all know what it is to see family and its members angry. Of course, we all should know it is healthy to feel guilty when our expressions of anger are undisciplined, destructive, or abusive.

We have seen that anger is experienced by God, who is Spirit, and His highest creation, mankind. To pretend that anger doesn't exist is unrealistic and even unhealthy.

Anger can appear to be a difficult emotion to define. In com-ing to a clear and understandable definition, we would do well to see anger as a rather complex entity yet definable and rec-ognizable.

Workbook: *Anger: Our Master or Our Servant,* Turning Point, P. O. Box 22127, Chattanooga, TN 37422-2127

Anger is generally felt as intense energy or a progressive surge of emotional energy that involves one's thoughts, feelings or emotions, and behaviors or actions. Thus in experiencing this feeling, we find it hard to separate these three parts.

• Anger Is Physiological

Dr. Richard D. Dobbins defines anger as *unexpressed energy*. A physiological response occurs when "a biochemical reaction is triggered which results in the creation of unusual amounts of energy for your use in facing a perceived threat. ... Once you are angry, you are in possession of energy which cannot be destroyed. Until you determine what form the expression of your energy will take, you have committed no sin. Your moral challenge is this: You are responsible to determine what you will do with the energy your anger has created" (82). So first of all, we see anger as a God-created energy, and we should not see anger as a sinful creation.

List ways in which you experience anger as a physiological phenomenon.

• Anger Involves Our Thoughts

The surge of energy we feel in our body is processed through mental, cognitive or thought processes. Whether we act out these strong feelings when anger occurs depends on our thoughts about the situations, ourselves, or others we see as stimulating our anger. Our mental attitude will determine our response to this energy.

How does a person's thoughts about a situation that makes them angry affect their response to it or to others when they are angry?

• Anger Is Action (Behavioral)

The words and actions people use (or do not use) to express the surge of anger they feel is the third component of anger. A broad range of expressions may occur.

There are a variety of expressions that reveal varying degrees of anger one can feel once they experience anger or react to a situation in anger.

A few of these are listed:

abhor	hot	resentful
annoyed	huffy	repulsed
begrudge	hurt	sarcastic
burned up with	ill-tempered	savage
cool to	incensed	scorn
cranky	indignant	sick of
criticize	inflamed	sore
cross	infuriated	spiteful
crushed	irked	testy
disdain	irritated	ticked off
disguised	jealous	to kid
despise	laugh at	touchy
enraged	loathe	troubled
exasperated	mad	turned off
fed up with	mean	uptight
frustrated	miffed	vexed
furious	moody	vicious
give someone grief	offended	worked up
griped	out of sorts	
grouchy	provoked	
grumpy		

To summarize, we see anger as a complex emotion that is composed of feeling, thoughts, and behaviors. This offers hope that anger can be a positive force for good and can be used as a constructive energy in the Christian life.

Anger can be used for good or evil. As part of our body's natural response system, it can be directed in positive ways. Let's open God's Word and gain insight into how He views anger and how it can be utilized to motivate people to do His will and purpose.

Spiritual-Awareness

It is interesting to discover the biblical words for anger. Two frequently used Greek words for anger are *thumus* and *orge*. *Thumus* means turbulent commotion, temper, rage. *Orge* describes a long-lasting attitude of revenge or resentment. Other words are used in Scripture to define anger.

The following scripture give examples of anger and its expression as seen in a variety of characters and situations: Scripture indicates anger can be a positive emotion that motivates a person to speak and do God's will and purpose.

Workbook: *Anger: Our Master or Our Servant*, Turning Point, P. O. Box 22127, Chattanooga, TN 37422-2127

❑ Exodus 32:19-25

❑ Judges 14:1-19

❑ Judges 15:1-5

❑ Judges 15:14-16

❑ I Samuel 15:10-31

❑ I Samuel 17

❑ John 2:13-25

❑ Acts 15:35-40

How do you see anger as a positive influence in your life and family?

Examine your understanding of anger as being a three-part entity: emotion, thought, action. Describe.

Make an effort this week to become more conscious of these three components as you experience anger in your life.

Workbook: *Anger: Our Master or Our Servant*, Turning Point, P. O. Box 22127, Chattanooga, TN 37422-2127

Session **3** *Anger: What Causes It?*

Meet with God

Personal Notes

For your personal quiet time with God, read the following passages from His Word: Romans 7:13-25 and Romans 8 (the entire chapter).

Ask God to help you evaluate the struggle you may have in controlling your anger. What does Paul say causes this?

In Romans 7:25 and Romans 8, what does God teach you about the solution to this struggle?

Meditate on where you are in your struggle to control your emotions, especially anger.

Self-Awareness

In looking at what causes anger, let us not forget what we have learned about anger up to this point. In summary, we have seen that anger can be viewed as a universal, human emotion that comes as standard equipment "on loan" from God. It is biological and is experienced by humans as a common feeling. It can be used for good or evil. Anger has a set of parts: (1) physiological, (2) emotional, and (3) cognitive(that is, related to our thought processes). It is experienced at all age levels by both Christians and non-Christians.

What makes people angry?

Over time then, we see that anger can be a learned response which can come from how our parents handled anger. Also, our view of each situation and our thinking or belief about ourselves, others, and the threat we are facing can often determine our response. So then the anger is ultimately ours! We can all respond to the biological surge of energy in a variety of ways, some of which we have learned or not learned in our upbringing.

Describe various expressions of anger that you have seen in others.

Is anger simply a biological or animalistic response?

How accurate is it to say that man is subject only to his passions and has no decision or responsibility as to how he responds in expressing his anger?

A variety of secular theories explore the causes of anger in man. Some say that aggression is purely biological and at odds with his psychological processes. Others say that biological and genetic structure, blood chemistry, or even brain damage or disease can cause anger.

Psychologists, behavioral scientists, sociologists, and others have researched and theorized about anger and its causes for many years. Perhaps some of this data is constructive in understanding man as a biological being; however, there is yet to be discovered a gene or hormone that can or will control a man's hate, marital conflict, war, murder, etc. Anger is caused by many other influences that are not physical alone.

Anger can be stimulated by external and internal factors to help simplify our discussion. A few external factors are: (1) Our childhood and what we learned about anger in us and our family (2) Our theology and what we were taught in our church and Sunday school, (3) Some types of vocations (For example, shift work where sleep deprivation occurs and high stress jobs and work situations.) (4) Everyday living, driving in heavy traffic, seasonal stress (vacation, Christmas), and (5) A person's over-all health, medications (some medications have side-effects that may stimulate anger).

What are some jobs and work situations that seem to stimulate anger?

List other situations that may cause anger.

Does heavy traffic always arouse anger?

• *Internal Factors That Stimulate Anger*

Various feelings and attitudes toward ourselves can produce anger.

How can feelings of low self-esteem, inferiority, and inadequacy produce anger?

 Workbook: *Anger: Our Master or Our Servant*, Turning Point, P. O. Box 22127, Chattanooga, TN 37422-2127

How does a perfectionist personality or tendency in a person complicate their struggle with anger in their life?

Other internal causes of anger could be feelings of guilt. We often express anger at ourselves or others if we are judged by others or become jealous of someone and feel guilty about it. Rejection, painful memories of our past, and "put downs" can produce feelings of resentment and hostility.

Our physical health, pain, recovery from surgery, illness, biochemical changes (premenstrual syndrome, puberty, pregnancy, etc.) can contribute to anger. Being aware of these causes can help a person better prepare to deal with anger if these stresses tend to arouse angry feelings.

Spiritual-Awareness

As simple as it may appear that anger can result from certain situations inside and outside of us, the Bible can help us locate the real causes of our human tendency to become angry and thus let anger master and control our lives.

❑ Genesis 3:1-7

❑ Genesis 4:1-8

❑ Jonah 4:1-9

❑ John 18:4-11

❑ Galatians 5:18-21

❑ Hebrews 12:14-15

It is clear that in our human nature and sinful desires we submit more readily to non-Scriptural ways of expressing our anger. Our awareness of this cause of anger will alert us to the primary source of sinful anger in our lives. As human beings, we are restless and unfulfilled in our desires to reach the potential we see in ourselves or our relationship with others. The sinful nature of man places limitations on his ability to have these natural desires and needs adequately met, so man stays frustrated and restless in this condition.

Even after someone accepts Jesus Christ as his personal Saviour, he will continue to struggle with the pull of this force on his new life in Christ. Read Galatians 5:16-17.

What are the results of living by the Spirit?

 **M**eet with God

Personal Notes

Schedule some time this week to study Ephesians 4, especially verses 26-32. As you begin this study on anger and when it is sinful, ask God to help you understand what is meant by sinning with your anger.

Are there places and situations where you "give place to the devil" by sinning with your anger? Where?

Let God teach you to discern these sinful places in your life and give you strength to deal with them.

Self-Awareness

Frank B. Minirth and Paul D. Meier state, "Whenever feeling any significant anger toward yourself, God, or anybody else, you will best handle that anger if you immediately analyze whether it is appropriate or inappropriate. You will gain insight into your anger" (149).

Read the following vignette.

Jane and George are wife and husband. Jane is the expressive partner in the marriage. Outgoing, friendly, and assertive, she is quick to express her opinions and her dissatisfactions about people or events in her life. Jane is also prone to sudden bursts of angry words and, in some cases, loud shouting and door slamming.

Her husband George is the opposite of his wife in many ways. A calm person with steady emotions, he is conscious of his image in public and, therefore, he strives to be in control of himself and his feelings. He seeks to avoid confrontations because he finds the feelings they raise in himself too uncomfortable. George rarely expresses his anger or disappointment in public, but occasionally loses his temper with his children.

In arguments with his wife, George seeks to remain calm and in control. He is afraid that displays of his own anger will further inflame his wife, making a bad situation worse. He tries to control himself in arguments with Jane, because her anger is a picture to him of what he does not want to be, visibly enraged and out of control. But George is angry inside. His anger remains unexpressed. He argues his case mentally after the main event, even muttering swear words, when his wife has stormed out of the room.

George and Jane illustrate two basic ways people tend to handle their anger feelings—rage and resentment—ways that have very few benefits. These styles spring, in part, from a person's own temperament and also as learned habits of anger response. Rage is the act of giving in to our feelings of anger and blowing up, usually verbally, although rage may also be manifest as swearing, screaming, criticizing, condemning, name calling, or throwing tantrums.

Resentment is the act of holding anger feelings inside. It is usually characterized by angry thoughts or unkind, unfriendly feelings in the presence of another. George, in the above example, may be slower to realize his problem than Jane, whose problem is on public display. In fact, Jane feels very guilty and ashamed of her anger at her family and she wants to change and improve her relationships. George, on the other hand, often feels self-righteous and believes that he is the injured party, since he did not "lose his cool." His inner resentments and bitterness are much more harmful than his wife's displays of anger, since he fails to recognize or deal with his problem.

Both of these styles of anger expression can be harmful and sinful, because they destroy human relationships. Both George and Jane are controlled by their feelings and neither is free to act in consciously thoughtful ways that seek to resolve problems and build relationships.

(*Counseling for Anger* by Mark P. Cosgrove, PhD., 1988. Word, Inc. Dallas, Texas. Used with permission.)

What does this vignette reveal about two basic styles of expressing anger?

Dr. Cosgrove points out that burying your anger or suppressing it may be the way many people handle their anger.

What are some expressions people use to describe this form of managing anger?

When we bury our anger inside, it may often result in holding it in or depositing it on another person or thing. This displacement can take a variety of forms such as avoiding the issue or person that angered you. You may reveal your anger in another form known as passive-aggressive behavior. Examples are: being late for work, picking on the kids or wife, dumping your anger at home, or even "kicking the cat." Being unresponsive to a situation or person may indicate that you are "holding in anger" toward them or some situation that involves them. This can build into a low level of resentment or bitterness. Sometimes it may be disguised as sarcasm, ridicule, or critical joking or humor.

Is it possible that a Christian could suppress his anger in the above ways we have seen as inappropriate because he feels anger is sinful and cannot be expressed? Describe.

In fact, the Bible teaches that resentment and bitterness are wrong; therefore, sin could develop from holding anger inside. The thoughts one has toward another that are not honestly expressed may result in a sinful expression that would not occur if the person had an honest, open leveling with others. To level with someone—self, God, or another—is to risk sharing your feelings in open, honest, carefrontation, rather than isolating your feelings. You may find it difficult to share your angry feelings with another, but it will help prevent sinful responses from occurring.

Carefully study the chart, *Development of Emotional Problems Related to Anger,* on page 24. After studying this chart, note other symptoms that can develop in a person if they hold anger inside.

This chart can also provide help in recognizing sinful patterns of anger. If you become preoccupied with the thoughts of hurts and losses and low self-esteem, energy is drained which can result in increased tension and bodily stress.

When a person holds anger inside, what other symptoms can possibly develop?

Workbook: *Anger: Our Master or Our Servant,* Turning Point, P. O. Box 22127, Chattanooga, TN 37422-2127

Development of Emotional Problems Related to Anger

Phase 1: Hurt
Bruised feelings from personal slight or disappointment.

Phase 2: Frustration
Feeling that comes when life tells you NO!

Phase 3: Fear
Feeling that comes with loss of control and anticipation of reprisal.

Phase 4: Anger
Feelings of hurt that are complicated by frustration and fear.

Phase 5: Wrath
Anger that has "brewed overnight" which gets stronger and grows into bitterness and unforgiveness.

Phase 6: Hostility
Anger collected and aggressive.

Phase 7: Hate
Bottled-up hostility which may be turned inward in depression or grow to the point of exploding into violence directed at one's self or toward the person or group that is blamed for the original hurt.

Recovery: To deal with anger, go back to the hurt, acknowledge the hurt, take responsibility for your part, and forgive the other person for their part.

By Dr. Raymond Brock. *Used by permission.*

The Bible tells us a great deal about holding anger in and how it can become a place for sin to develop and thus provide a place for Satan to create a stronghold.

✓ Reference	Notes from the Reading
❏ Ephesians 4:31	
❏ Ephesians 4:30	
❏ Ephesians 4:32	
❏ II Samuel 12:1-25	
❏ Psalm 42:3,5,10	
❏ Psalm 38:4	
❏ Psalm 51:1-6	
❏ Matthew 7:3-5	
❏ Mark 11:25-26	
❏ Romans 12:19	
❏ Colossians 3:21	

Workbook: *Anger: Our Master or Our Servant*, Turning Point, P. O. Box 22127, Chattanooga, TN 37422-2127

In the Old Testament passages listed for your study, David wrestled with facing his sin and the resulting anger.

What can you learn from David and his experience with anger as recorded in these passages?

Depression can be a hiding place for anger. In fact, when we hide anger, it can lead to depression. When situations anger us and we push the feeling down inside, it can lead us on a temporary trip into self-hatred. Very often suicidal persons are unaware of their anger at themselves. In counseling, I have often asked a severely depressed counselee who may be contemplating suicide,"Are you aware of your anger at yourself?" They will often respond with a question: "Why do you think I am angry with myself?" I reply,"It seems to me that before you would want to kill someone, you would have to become very angry at them—even if that someone is you!" In many cases, suicide is believed to be associated with depression that is severe. Depression is often a result of repeated episodes of long-term, hidden anger. Getting in touch with it and revealing it to God and a person whom you can trust will often bring help in relieving the depression.

David was depressed in these passages in the Psalms.

How did his sin with Bathsheba and the other sins that followed plus the harassment of his enemies contribute to his anger and depression?

Can you see how sin leads to anger and depression?

Burying anger can lead to sinful thoughts and behaviors. We need to become aware of our tendency to bury or hide it. The church has often allowed Christians to identify with the pain of their hurtful feelings and pain of the past but not with their anger. In this group it's safe to say, "I'm hurt," but it's even better to say, "I'm angry!"

Hopefully at this point in the group, bonding and trust should have developed to the point where you can share some of your anger that may be displaced onto others or buried inside and hidden from others. **Describe.**

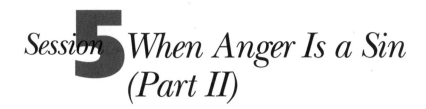

Session 5 When Anger Is a Sin (Part II)

Meet with God

Personal Notes

In your quiet time with God this week, spend time reading and studying Galatians 5:16-26. Seek to discover how you can make progress spiritually in the truth you find in this very important passage of scripture. Explore how to *walk in the Spirit* and its application for managing anger in your life.

Self-Awareness

In our last session, we explored the dangers and benefits of choosing to hide or repress our anger. In some cases, to stuff our anger can result in sinful expressions of anger; i.e., resentment and bitterness. In other cases, to control the anger by holding it in and releasing it or letting it go without hurting ourselves or others may be beneficial. In this session we will explore a common way that anger is often expressed, one that could be and in many cases is not the most appropriate way to do so.

What does it mean for us to *vent* our anger or lose our temper? List some words or phrases often used to describe this.

We know that anger can be internalized and/or externalized in harmful or beneficial ways. We have viewed the dangers of unhealthy *hiding* of anger. Let's look at the dangers of exploding or venting anger in explosive episodes. As we will see in our Spiritual Awareness segment of this session, that the Bible clearly teaches that open hostility, loss of temper, violent acts, retaliation, and the aggressive expression of anger are not appropriate for the Christian. A person who loses control of his anger can be mastered by it and act with violent behavior. Aggression that explodes in thoughtless anger can hurt ourselves and others.

When we vent our anger on family, friends, or strangers, negative results occur such as:

1) Problems are not solved when we vent our anger on others or lash out at them. In fact, it often intensifies hostility.

2) Others who are the target of open rage and explosive anger are hurt emotionally and, in some cases, physically. (Each year millions of children are battered by out-of-control parents, and spouses are abused by their mates.) Anger and

rage often control the emotions of street gangs in our cities. Our pastor told of a recent television program where he watched interviews with street gang members. One of these members blatantly remarked that he would immediately murder anyone who just looked at his trousers in the wrong way or if he just didn't like the way they looked. That is all it took for him to kill another human being. He further remarked that he got a thrill out of watching the blood spurt out of their body! This may seem like an extreme example of violent anger, but many of these gang members acted "controlled" and "cool" as they reported this. Anger, revenge, and hatred produce negative and hurtful results.

3) Anger that is released in violent ways does not change others. It may appear that they have changed when threatened through angry aggression, but ultimately, respect, love, and warm feelings decrease. Vented anger does not get good results in others.

4) When people explode or vent their anger inappropriately, it does not help them better express, control, or accept their anger. The opposite tends to occur. Their restraints on releasing anger often diminish, and they accept this aggressive temper as okay. This tends to keep them in a state of anger that helps perpetuate a cycle of anger, guilt over losing control and hurting others, recurrent anger, recurrent guilt, etc. (This pattern is seen in those who abuse others verbally or physically). People do not listen well when someone is inappropriately releasing anger.

In general, what is the prevailing attitude of people who dump or openly release their anger on others?

Is there a difference between irritation and rage?

Oliver and Wright in *When Anger Hits Home* quote John Lee on how devastating rage can be:

> *Rage is the ugliest and meanest human emotion. Rage is the father throwing his infant child against the wall and killing her. Rage is the mother scalding her child with boiling water to teach a lesson. Rage is the husband choking the family dog because it sneaked into the house. Rage is the driver who tailgates you for 10 miles blowing his horn because you cut him off by mistake... Rage is awful and has no decent place in normal human relationships. Not at home. Not at work. Not in public (224).*

Think about the following statement for a moment: "Is there any difference between people who get angry and angry people?" Describe.

Workbook: *Anger: Our Master or Our Servant*, Turning Point, P. O. Box 22127, Chattanooga, TN 37422-2127

It is clear that the extreme expression of anger as seen in rage, violent outbursts, or verbal or physical abuse of others provides a negative and harmful release of this powerful emotion.

The following scriptures show us that venting anger inappropriately can be sinful.

✓	Reference	Notes from the Reading
❏	Proverbs 15:1	
❏	Proverbs 15:18	
❏	Proverbs 16:28	
❏	Proverbs 22:24	
❏	Mark 3:17	
❏	Luke 9:49-56	
❏	Romans 12:17	
❏	Colossians 3:8	
❏	Colossians 3:12-14	

We have seen that it is always inappropriate to vent our anger on ourselves or others. Any expression of anger that abuses others is not biblical. Look over the following list of indicators that may need your attention. Perhaps some changes are in order. **Did you discover any areas that apply to you?**

Think about these and ask the Lord to help you come to terms with your discovery. Get assertive with changes that are needed in your dealing with explosive anger. **If even one of these indicators fits you, target it for change! Describe.**

Oliver and Wright in *When Anger Hits Home* record this quote: "In *Treating Type A Behavior and Your Heart,* Friedman and Ulmer identified certain behaviors that, based on research, may be indicators of a hostile personality. According to Dr. Friedman, if even one descriptor fits you, it may be time to contend with your tendency toward hostility.

1. "You become irritated or angry at relatively minor mistakes of family members, friends, acquaintances, or even complete strangers or find such mistakes hard to overlook.

2. "You frequently find yourself critically examining a situation in order to find something that is wrong or might go wrong.

3. "You find yourself scowling and unwilling or unable to laugh at things your friends laugh at.

4. "You are overly proud of your ideas and enjoy telling others about them.

5. "You frequently find yourself thinking or saying that most people cannot be trusted.

6. "You find yourself regarding even one person with contempt.

7. "You have a regular tendency to shift the subject of a conversation to the errors of large corporations, of various departments and offices of the federal government, or to the younger generation.

8. "You frequently use obscenities in your speech.

9. "You find it difficult to compliment or congratulate other people with honest enthusiasm." (225-226.)

Workbook: *Anger: Our Master or Our Servant,* Turning Point, P. O. Box 22127, Chattanooga, TN 37422-2127

Session **6** *Beginning Steps in Managing Your Anger*

Meet With God

Personal Notes

Spend 30 minutes each day in meditation and prayer. Study James 3. This chapter in the Bible has much to say about the importance of using your tongue wisely or managing your speech. Ask God to help you gain insight into the importance of how to manage anger, especially the words you use to express it. Pray and meditate on the truths you discover in the direct instruction from God's Word about your tongue.

Self-Awareness

It is understood that people can have a number of misconceptions about their feelings. Are their feelings right or wrong? Do I hold my feelings inside or do I release them? Where do my feelings come from: God or Satan? Can I trust them?

Feelings, of course, are an indispensable part of our lives. Anger is one of the feelings about which many of the above questions are often asked. As a person learns that he is a person "with feelings," he may appear confused about them, disregard them, or even deny his feelings, especially if the feeling is one of anger.

Feelings are a God-given gift. They are like guides to help us sense or monitor issues and events in our lives. They provide a part of the total response mechanism God created in us so we can be motivated to better understand, evaluate, judge, and respond to situations and circumstances in our lives. Although feelings should not be the final criteria that determine our behavioral responses or decisions, they still provide a vital part of the total information we need to help us be the person God wants us to be in serving Him and others.

It is tragic if we lose our ability to be in touch with our feelings. It is almost like we are losing one of our senses such as sight, touch, or smell. To know or recognize your feelings is like being in touch with a "sixth sense" that provides a valuable tool in helping us experience life to the fullest, especially in relationship with God and others. This is especially true with regard to the feelings of anger we experience.

Describe ways we are *not* to handle anger.

In preparing to manage anger properly, we know that to deny our feelings, repress them, and/or explode and throw them at others can result in a sinful use of this powerful energy God created in us to use in a productive way. Also in preparation for managing anger, we need to remember that God's Word provides some very important guidelines or principles that will help us understand this powerful emotion and His purpose and plan for using it appropriately. As we have already seen, the Bible presents a variety of statements, words, and situations that involve the emotion of anger.

By now we should be fairly certain from our study that anger is a subject the Bible readily addresses. However, in learning to manage our anger, we need to become aware of some specific truths that God's Word shows us about anger.

When we take time to explore the Bible thoroughly on anger management we discover something interesting. It seems as if the Bible says in some passages that anger is condemned and other times that anger is condoned.

Spiritual-Awareness

It is clear that the Scriptures give us some key truths for managing our anger.

Workbook: *Anger: Our Master or Our Servant*, Turning Point, P. O. Box 22127, Chattanooga, TN 37422-2127

❑ Psalm 37:8 and Ephesians 4:31

❑ Psalm 4:4 and Ephesians 4:26

❑ Genesis 1:26-27

❑ Ecclesiastes 7:9

❑ Ephesians 4:26-27

❑ II Samuel 6:6-8

❑ Acts 13:22

❑ Numbers 11:1

❑ Mark 11:15-17

❑ Numbers 25:16-17

❑ I Samuel 11:6

1. The Bible teaches we are to be slow to anger; however, these verses teach us we must not delay showing our anger any longer than is necessary. If you have to express anger, it is important to deal with that expression appropriately and quickly. Don't wait for days, weeks, months, or years to pass before talking with someone you may have hurt or reacted to in anger. To delay could cause greater pain for you and them.
2. Deal with anger the same day it occurs.
3. Deal with your anger while there is opportunity to do so. Don't let it stockpile in a slush fund of repressed and denied angry feelings.
4. When you are angry, deal with it or you may become vulnerable and give Satan a place to use you and your anger in sinful expressions of thought and behavior.
5. Don't let lingering anger proceed to bitterness and resentment.

Ask God to help you understand these truths and apply them to your life.

It may help you to note that many well-known Bible characters had to deal with anger. They often expressed their anger at God and others. Dr. Dwight Carlson in his book, *Overcoming Hurts and Anger*, states:

> *Do you know who in the Bible got angry the most often? Not the Pharisees, or the Philistines, nor any other assorted heathen. It was God Himself–God, who is without sin. The Hebrew word for anger appears approximately 455 times in the Old Testament, and of these, 375 times it is referring to the anger of God"* (35).

Therefore, we can conclude that anger as seen in the Scriptures is presented in and of itself as neutral, neither right nor wrong, appropriate nor inappropriate. The Bible teaches us that it is what makes us angry(the source or basis of our anger) and how it is expressed that determines whether anger is right or wrong.

Application

Anger is a powerful, God-created energy that can be utilized in a sinful or righteous expression. It may be helpful to review Session Two briefly, especially the components of anger. As you have read God's Word, prayed, shared, and let God's Holy Spirit search your heart, hopefully you have come to understand that the creative use of anger must first be understood in the light of Scripture, and the basic principle of how to manage it must be developed from God's Word.

Describe ways anger can be expressed within the boundaries of the Scripture.

Describe some personal applications.

Workbook: *Anger: Our Master or Our Servant*, Turning Point, P. O. Box 22127, Chattanooga, TN 37422-2127

Session 7 Managing Your Anger

Personal Preparation: Getting Ready for Session Seven

Meet with God

Personal Notes

Inappropriate use of anger can result in sin. Ask God to help you develop constructive ways of dealing with anger. Place special emphasis on studying and meditating on new ways to express anger gleaned from James 1:12-23. Also meditate on James 5:16. You may also want to deepen your study by reading Psalm 55, 57, and 58 to determine how David expressed his feelings in a variety of ways: verbally, by writing them down, etc. **How "in touch" are you with your feelings of anger and the ways you express them?** Seek insight from God's Word.

Self-Awareness

In developing a healthy viewpoint of our feelings, it is necessary that we come to terms with anger. This emotion must be the focus or target of our concern if we are to mature in our self-control and development as a growing Christian.

As we have already seen, there seems to be two common responses to anger; denial or stuffing/burying it and/or venting it and displaying aggressive, explosive temper tantrums.

The Bible clearly states we are to practice "being slow to anger" (James 1:19). This simple admonition means we can work with angry feelings, not just bury them or release them in bursts of temper. In this session we will provide a simple plan for learning how to be *slow to anger;* i.e., learn how to take control, manage, and utilize anger in productive ways. The following step-by-step procedure provides clear-cut steps to help you control the episodes of anger that come into your life:

1. ***Get in touch with your feelings.*** Acknowledge your feelings of anger and accept them. Describe your feelings: *I am mad. I am irritated. I am furious.* Determine the level and intensity of these feelings: a little upset, moderately upset, or very upset. Get honest with your anger. Admit you are losing control. At this point don't be critical of your feelings as to their being right or wrong but look at your feelings and think of them as you would a temperature gauge on the dash of your automobile. The gauge light comes on, and is red indicating

that the engine is overheated. You do not try to determine the cause of the malfunction nor try to fix it at this point. You just observe the warning light. It's overheated! Just acknowledge the fact. That is the principle of this first step in controlling your anger. Just acknowledge and accept the fact of feeling angry. Don't deny it!

Give an example.

2. Control your thoughts. In doing this, you will be able to control and determine what to say or do. Alert yourself and others to the fact that you are displeased, angry, or upset. Don't take any actions on your immediate feelings. Be truthful with yourself and others. You may respond by saying, "What you said to me upset me; however, I need to think through my response to you. Maybe we need to talk about this after I clear my thoughts and feelings." Be aware of the situation that angered you but defer specific action until you think about how to respond as well as how it has affected your feelings. Timing your response is important. Prayer will definitely help you clarify the issue and how you are to deal with it.

Give an example.

3. Locate the cause of your anger. Ask yourself, "What is it that is making me angry?" Sort out what you caused and what others did to produce the anger. Discern the root cause of problem. If you get angry because the car will not start, is it truly that the car won't start, or is it fear of being late and your boss's getting angry at you. Or could it be that you are angry that if the car is broken, it will cause additional financial worry and stress? Over time, you can begin to locate the true cause of your anger. Accept responsibility for your anger and process the information to locate a cause. For further study in this particular step of anger management, you may want to read *The Anger Workbook* by Dr. Les Carter and Dr. Frank Minirth (see Bibliography). The workbook provides valuable help in discerning how a variety of needs; e.g., insecurity, fear, pride, loneliness, inferiority, and unrealistic expectations can create anger.

Give an example.

4. Think through your response by being rational and less emotional. Spend time sorting out irrational beliefs. Tell yourself the truth about people and situations. No one is ever wrong or right all the time. It is wrong to expect others to always be happy and helpful. People do get sick, tired, and aged. Others have reasons for their behaviors and are not just selfish or thoughtless. Everyone and everything does not exist for our convenience or purpose. You will control anger better if you do not say, *I can't stand this...,* or *They should or shouldn't do this...,* or *They better never....* These statements lock

Workbook: *Anger: Our Master or Our Servant,* Turning Point, P. O. Box 22127, Chattanooga, TN 37422-2127

you into emotionalizing rather than thinking. Align yourself with reality and don't let everything bother you to the point that you "lose it" every time over normal failures we all have and experience as a result of being imperfect and having a fallen, sinful nature. Note: This does not mean we don't deal with the reality of sin and wrong, but to be "slow to anger" means we are relating to life through self-control, grace, and understanding.

Give an example.

5. Direct your anger through applied controls. In determining your course of action, remember to avoid the extremes that could be harmful: attacking, withdrawing and clamming up, giving in, or denying anger that is present.

If you care for someone or some situation, you will often have to choose action that requires that you confront someone or some event. David Augsburger in his book, *Caring Enough To Confront,* calls this "truthing it in love." This action may be needed. You may need to be gentle and private with confrontation or strong and direct—whatever is needed to help bring a resolution to the conflict. In this process of "truthing it in love," be sure to do the following: (a) inform about the issue (b) show your feelings appropriately, and (c) speak the truth in love.

With God's help, carefully choose the proper response, words, action, and what to say or not to say to bring some closure and resolution to the issue. Develop a list of responses and actions that work for you and for the best of other people. It is at this level that anger becomes your servant and can be productive for you.

Give an example.

This simple five-part formula for controlling your anger will help you develop some basic control and give you a plan that can bring about management of it.

Spiritual-Awareness

The Apostle Paul says, "All Scripture is God-breathed and is useful for teaching, rebuking, correcting and training in righteousness" (II Timothy 3:16). Let's look at useful ways to apply the scripture.

❑ Matthew 5:22

❑ Matthew 16:23

❑ Acts 15:2

❑ Galatians 2:11

❑ Proverbs 25:8-9

❑ Ecclesiastes 7:21-22

❑ James 1:19

*A*pplication

Managing anger and using it for good requires practical as well as spiritual effort. Write out the five steps suggested in this session for controlling anger. Work on the ones you need to practice this week in your progression toward making anger your servant.

Read the James 1:19 passage. Describe what it means to you in terms of developing a plan to avoid the destructive use of anger.

Study carefully the *Anger Log* and *Anger Expression Charts on* pages 40 and 41. Commit yourself to using it for nine days to record your responses. This tool is quite valuable in helping you pinpoint angry reactions and their intensity. This discipline will pay great dividends in learning to be slow to anger. After nine days, compare with Session 1. **Describe your progress.**

My Anger Log									
Day	1	2	3	4	5	6	7	8	9
Frequency How many times do you get angry each day inwardly or outwardly? Place a number for each day.									
Intensity On the average, from 1-10 what is the intensity of your anger today? (10 = intense; 1= barely breathing)									
Duration How many minutes do you usually remain angry? Use an average.									
Negative Expression How many times does your anger lead to negative expression?									
Positive Expression How many times does your anger lead to positive expression?									
Disturbs Relationships On the average, did your anger today help or hinder relationships? (9= helpful; 1 =disaster)									

Fill out the Anger Expressions chart. Consider the last two times you got angry at each person and how you expressed it. Now observe how you express your anger the next time you get angry at each person.

ANGER EXPRESSIONS

✍ **Mark with a check (✓) how you expressed anger to each person most recently.**

Person	Hold it back	Indirect	Direct
Spouse	_____	_____	_____
Children	_____	_____	_____
Parents	_____	_____	_____
Employer	_____	_____	_____
Coworker	_____	_____	_____
Friends	_____	_____	_____

Which type of expression do you tend to use most?

What can you do to make your anger expression healthier and more productive?

✍ **Think about the following people toward whom you might express anger. How do they respond when you express anger? Write down how you will respond the next time.**

Person	Response	How I will respond differently the next time
Spouse	_____	_____
Children	_____	_____
Mother	_____	_____
Father	_____	_____
Boss	_____	_____
Friends	_____	_____

✍ **Think of a constant provoking behavior or situation and then think of a change that you can make when all else fails.**

Charts taken from *When Anger Hits Home* by Gary Jackson Oliver and H. Norman Wright. 1992. Moody Press. Used by permission.

Workbook: *Anger: Our Master or Our Servant*, Turning Point, P. O. Box 22127, Chattanooga, TN 37422-2127

Session 8 Managing Anger in Your Marriage and/or Family Relationships

Meet With God

Make a special effort to think about the place anger plays in your marriage and or family relationships. As you spend time with God this week, focus on the following scriptures: Ephesians 5:22-33 and I Corinthians 13.

What does God say about marriage in these passages, and what kind of love is needed ?

Self-Awareness

It is realistic to expect that most couples will experience anger in their marriage and with their children. We need to have adequate and accurate information in dealing with anger in our marriage and families. Disagreements and conflicts are inevitable. Marriage forces us to come to terms with our spouse's needs and submit our weaknesses to another person. If you are an intense person you can experience intensity in pain and/or pleasure. The area of anger in marriage is such a broad topic, David Mace, a pioneer in the field of marriage enrichment, has described its proper place in marriage.

This does not mean you do not have a right to be angry. In an appropriate situation, your anger could be a lifesaver. Anger enables us to assert ourselves in situations where we should. Anger exposes antisocial behavior in others. Anger gets wrongs righted. In a loving marriage, however, these measures are not necessary.

My wife is not my enemy. She is my best friend; and it does not help either of us if I treat her as an enemy. So I say, "I'm angry with you. But I don't like myself in this condition. I don't want to strike you. I'd rather stroke you." This renouncing of anger on one side prevents the rush of retaliatory anger on the other side, and the resulting tendency to drift into what I call the "artillery duel." If I present my state of anger against my wife as a problem I have, she is not motivated to respond angrily. Instead of a challenge to fight, it is an invitation to negotiate.

Taken from *When Anger Hits Home* by Gary Jackson Oliver and H. Norman Wright, 1992. Moody Press. Used by Permission.

Can you remember the first episode of anger you had as a married couple or family member?

The following areas seem to be the battlegrounds of anger: unfulfilled expectations, unfulfilled needs, differences in backgrounds, the way we give and receive love, money, sex, communication, parenting, in-laws, taking your spouse for granted, fatigue and time pressures, physical demands, job stress, sleep deprivation, dual careers, ad infinitum.

Power and control seem to be the overriding issues that lock couples into endless war, and like the game of "tug-o-war," they will stubbornly continue to fight for their victory, and anger is a vital energy used to achieve it. The biblical concept of marriage is built on the principle of submission to one another in love. But does this involve conflict? Yes! In a healthy marriage a couple experiences conflict from time to time. The marriage commitment requires you to look at your self or selfishness and your mate's self or selfishness. Thus, what "he wants" and "she wants" and what "he needs" and "she needs" and what "he expects" and "she expects" erupt in disagreements and arguments. In our culture we favor independence and self-reliance. Little value is placed on cooperation, flexibility, and giving in to achieve a greater goal. Yet we all struggle with problems we cannot solve by ourselves. Growth and maturity develop as we work through problems and conflicts together. Removing ourselves from the issue or our mate may mean less anger, but it always lessens the intimacy and potential for the couple's growth. Mark Cosgrove in *Counseling for Anger* states, "So many marriages fail, not because people have married the wrong people, but because they are not *being* the right people" (107).

We need the freedom in our marriages where anger and hurt can be expressed properly and in a loving, truthful manner. Feelings must be expressed to one another without fear of rejection and yet without hurting your spouse.

Name two areas in your marriage or family that seem to stimulate angry episodes between family members.

Workbook: *Anger: Our Master or Our Servant*, Turning Point, P. O. Box 22127, Chattanooga, TN 37422-2127

Disagreements are normal and even inevitable in marriage. Consider the following to help you and your spouse use anger constructively in your marriage.

- Learn how to manage conflict by admitting you are angry.

- First, deal with your anger.

- Practice the skills learned in the previous session.

- Commit yourself to "being slow to get angry."

- Ask yourself: "How will the presence of Jesus Christ in my life affect the way I respond to my mate and this situation?"

- Learn how to hold back your anger. Think ahead to avoid anger-causing situations.

- Make up your mind not to let everything bother you. Self-giving love means you will do what you can to remove irritating situations and unnecessary conflict from your spouse's life if at all possible.

- Purpose in your heart not to overreact, threaten, hit, curse, shout at, or call names with your mate. There will be times when each of you may need to discover a *set of techniques* that you will use (agreeable to both) to rely on that will help diffuse the intensity of your heated moments of dialogue. Some couples use *time out* to get control of their impulses or feelings, others count to ten, others change the scene or subject to allow calmness to return so the issue can be addressed later.

What methods have you used to control anger in your marriage or family?

Whenever a married couple cannot reach a resolution to an angry conflict, it is often due to the fact that one or both of them have sabotaged their dialogue or communication. Good communication skills require practice. Couples often *fight in dirty ways* that block communication and increase anger.

A simple tool a couple can use to avoid these episodes and better manage them is to agree on a simple *communication covenant* or prior agreement as to how they will **act** during their disagreements. I like the example from Gary Oliver and Norman Wright's book, *When Anger Hits Home* (167-168).

Here are two points from an agreement that one couple developed in order to improve their communication and problem-solving skills.
1. We will not exaggerate or attack the other person during the course of a disagreement.
   a. I will stick with the specific issue.
   b. I will take several seconds to formulate words so that I can be accurate.

     c   *I will consider the consequences of what I say before I say it.*

     d. *I will not use the words always, all the time, everyone, nothing, etc.*

2. *We will attempt to control the emotional level and intensity of arguments. (No yelling, uncontrollable anger, hurtful remarks.)*

     a. *We will take time-outs for calming down if either of us feels that our own anger is starting to elevate too much. The minimum amount of time for a time-out will be one minute and the maximum ten minutes. The person who needs a greater amount of time in order to calm down will be the one to set the time limit. During the time-out, each person, individually and in writing, will first of all define the problem that is being discussed. This will include, first, identifying the specific cause for my anger. Second, the areas of agreement in the problem will be listed. Third, the areas of disagreement will be listed, and fourth, three alternate solutions to this problem will be listed. When we come back together, the person who has been the most upset will express to the other individual, "I'm interested in what you've written during our time-out. Will you share yours with me?"*

     b. *Before I say anything, I will decide if I would want this same statement said to me with the same words and tone of voice.*

It is most helpful for couples to support one another in keeping their *communication covenant* or agreement. Ask each other what is needed to control angry feelings. For example: Ask "Do you want me to say nothing, leave the room, not interrupt, hold you, hear you out, etc., when you are losing or about to lose control of your anger?" Reflect and ask questions. Ask yourself: "How can I make this process work?" Both spouses must be in the process or agreement together and help each other make it work.

List ways you would want your loved one to respond to you when you are angry.

Workbook: *Anger: Our Master or Our Servant*, Turning Point, P. O. Box 22127, Chattanooga, TN 37422-2127

As couples grow in their management skills, they will know when to keep quiet about trivial matters and when to argue for the sake of things important to the relationship. Learning how to handle marital storms is more than just learning "techniques for conflict resolution," communication skills, etc. These will only help a couple's skills in dealing with anger. The greatest factor in learning to manage anger in a marriage is to see that self-control is a character issue. Our study on anger is to help us become more loving and less selfish in our relationships. Our marriages can be destroyed by many forces, but one of them that does not have to end it is anger. Solutions to anger in marriage cannot be reduced to a list of *how-tos*. People need to change on the inside if they are to develop loving, caring, nonabusive relationships.

Spiritual-Awareness

The biblical principles of how the marriage relationship is to function will provide a greater resource for maintaining a healthy marriage which will also help us with proper anger management.

Submitting to "one another out of reverence for Christ" (Ephesians 5:21) involves anger management in marriage and family relationships.

❏ Psalm 103:8

❏ Matthew 5:38-42

❏ Ephesians 5:22-33

❏ Colossians 3:13

❏ Romans 14:13

❏ Galatians 6:2

Workbook: *Anger: Our Master or Our Servant*, Turning Point, P. O. Box 22127, Chattanooga, TN 37422-2127

Read this quote and think about how you and your spouse deal with anger. Perhaps you can commit yourself to the Biblical principle of *holding back* your anger so that God can accomplish His purpose in each of your lives.

Couples who are mature in their handling of anger and conflict know when to keep quiet about trivial matters and when to argue for the sake of things important to the relationship. It is often sound advice to do nothing about being irritated or angry at one's spouse. There are too many irritations and conflicts of interest in marriage to get angry at every one of them. What people should not do is to wear their spouses out with the continued expression of trivial angers so that important matters are ignored when they arise. On the benefits of holding anger back, Carol Tavris writes,

> *In the final analysis, managing anger depends on taking responsibility for one's emotions and one's actions: on refusing the temptation, for instance, to remain stuck in blame or fury or silent resentment. Once anger becomes a force to berate the nearest scapegoat instead of to change a bad situation, it only loses its credibility and its power. It feeds only on itself. And it sure as sunrise makes for a grumpy life.*

It would be hard to say more clearly that holding anger back can be very positive; but perhaps the words of Scripture say it best: "a gentle answer turns away wrath..." (Proverbs 15:1) .

(*Counseling for Anger* by Mark P. Cosgrove, PhD., 1988. Word, Inc. Dallas, Texas. Used with permission.)

According to Proverbs 15:1, how can we prevent anger from escalating out of control?

Session 9 Accepting Responsibility for Managing My Anger

Meet with God

Personal Notes

As you come to the end of this study on *Anger: Our Master or Our Servant,* hopefully you have gained some insights and made some decisions about how to use the gift of anger as your servant. Change is often difficult for us as we discover a truth that needs to become a part of our life, especially if it requires the effort of making specific changes in the way we feel, think, or act. In your quiet time this week, spend time in prayer asking God to help you do what He wants you to do in controlling anger in all of your relationships. After allowing His Spirit to speak to you about this, covenant with Him and your fellow group members that you will be accountable to Him and at least one other person in the group to make the effort to take your responsibility to make anger your servant, not let it master you or your life.

Review various scripture passages in the previous sessions that relate specifically to the areas that God has spoken to you about changing. Study them in your quiet time this week.

Self-Awareness

Ten Steps in Anger Preventative Maintenance

As we come to the conclusion of our study on controlling anger in our lives, we should begin to see progress in making anger our servant. As you have worked at accepting your anger and are developing your skills in anger management, hopefully growth is beginning to take place.

When our two sons were children, very often I would hear one of them say to the other in a whiny tone as a put-down, "Oh, why don't you **grow up**!" It was used skillfully as a manipulative statement to get that brother to stop something or to get something done. "You are acting like a baby" was often heard, too.

God wants us to grow up. Of course, He does not say it in a manipulative, whiny tone of voice, nor does he humiliate or put us down.

Workbook: *Anger: Our Master or Our Servant,* Turning Point, P. O. Box 22127, Chattanooga, TN 37422-2127

In our Spiritual Awareness section we will see that God's Word encourages us to become Christlike and mature. Anger management is ultimately a function of spiritual maturity. As we grow and develop in our relationship with God by living a consistent Christian life, we will be able to control our anger and use it as a gift from God. This takes time, discipline, and often requires help from others to whom we are accountable for our growth.

In our study we have discovered the definition of anger, causes of anger, and the various responses we can make in feeling, thought, and action with anger. We now come to terms with the way we accept responsibility for controlling our anger. It is important to consider ways not only to control anger but also actually take steps to prevent it. We must work on controlling anger when we are in quiet periods and not angry. Some suggestions for balancing our lives so we don't misuse anger or sin with it are listed below. Apply these during times of less conflict and reduced anger. As a friend of mine says, *"Strike when the iron is cold, not hot."* This helps you better manage the *hot* times when anger rears its head.

1. *Keep your life balanced and purposeful.* Maintain goals in your life—physical, spiritual, intellectual, and social. Stay active.

2. *Don't neglect your physical health, diet, rest, diversion from routine.* Plan times to enjoy God's beauty outdoors. Reading good books, meditation, quiet times, and healthy walks and talks with family and friends help lower anger levels. Develop an appropriate hobby.

3. *Spend time with God, His Word, and in prayer.* Cultivate a quiet time each day that will help you develop God's character in your life.

4. *Avoid overloads of stress.* When crisis comes, learn how to react emotionally in ways that will help you better cope. We are more susceptible to anger when depressed, fearful, or even happy and elated.

5. *Be realistic in your expectations of self and others.* Sometimes we expect too much of ourselves and others. One of the quickest ways to overcome hurt and anger, even prevent it, is to check your expectations. Are they appropriate and realistic? List those things that upset you, irritate you. Look at the list. Are the needs and expectations legitimate? Be honest. Deal with those that are unrealistic in yourself and others; otherwise, you will continue to become angry over them.

6. *Guard your tongue and speech.* Practice the art of listening. Listen to your self-talk. Are you negative and self-pitying? Are you critical of self and others? Let God help you learn to control your tongue.

7. *Do not compare yourself to others.* Learn to accept others and their gifts and talents. You do not have to compete with others. Use this creative energy to be productive, not jealous, angry, and bitter at others' successes and abilities. God created you! Be yourself!

8. *Avoid angry people and anger-provoking situations you are not prepared to handle.* Be cautious not to stimulate anger this way. Remove yourself from people and/or situations until you have matured enough in patience, control, and honesty as well as wisdom in responding to them.

9. *Let go of old deposits of anger—forgive and forget.* If you are harboring old hurts and residual anger, resentments that are unresolved, deal with them. As a Christian, you are a "new person in Christ." However, old wounds can still hurt. Heal them through asking God and others for forgiveness. Forgive—choose to give up the held grudge. Stop licking old wounds. Forgiving does not mean we minimize the hurt or injury inflicted on us. Whatever the case, we must forgive them and ourselves.

   The other alternatives are to hold it in, deny it hurts, become bitter or resentful, or even attack, none of these effectively get rid of pent-up anger.

   Practice this in every area of your life. Keep short accounts of anger, and your life will be less angry.

10. *Work on improving your relationships to reduce anger in them.* Plant seeds of peace, joy, and self-control with those near you. Great dividends will be paid tomorrow for today's effort.

Which of the *Ten Steps* is most difficult for you? Describe.

Keep setting personal growth goals to improve, mature, and become the person God wants you to become each day.

 Workbook: *Anger: Our Master or Our Servant*, Turning Point, P. O. Box 22127, Chattanooga, TN 37422-2127

Spiritual-Awareness

The ten ways to prevent anger we have just studied originate
in God's Word. The following passages provide information
and inspiration to reach the goal of controlling anger:

✓	Reference	Notes from the Reading
❏	Exodus 20:10	
❏	Psalm 16:9	
❏	Isaiah 30:15	
❏	Isaiah 40:31	
❏	Mark 6:30-31	
❏	Matthew 6:15	
❏	Matthew 18:21-35	
❏	Philippians 2:12-14	

❑ Philippians 4:4-7

_____

❑ Philippians 4:12-13

_____

❑ James 3:3-12

_____

❑ Hebrews 6:1-3

After reading the parable of the *unmerciful servant* (Matthew 18:21-35), ask yourself the following questions about forgiveness:

1. Who has extended forgiveness to you?
2. To whom have you given a lot of forgiveness?
3. When you forgive others, how does it affect you?
4. How do you forgive people who don't know they have offended you?
5. How important is the practice of forgiveness in helping you control your anger?
6. How can a constant state of forgiveness prevent anger?

After reading James 3:3-12, think about these questions and answer them honestly:

1. Is it easy for you to control your tongue?
2. How does controlling your tongue keep others from exploding in anger?
3. How does slow, kind, and soft speech, even silence, calm you and others, and prevent anger from controlling you?

We began this session with the importance of maturing or growing up in Christ. **If anger is basically a spiritual problem, what are God's goal and desire for us in growing up with regard to managing anger?**

In getting control over anger in your life, be patient. This is not easily accomplished in one step or by memorizing the techniques we have suggested. However, every step toward your goal will bring you closer to it.

As we have seen, anger is a potential force created by God for productive use in our lives. Take this energy and use it and multiply it. Let anger not only be your friend but also make it your servant—make it God's servant. God can help you manage anger and use it for His glory.

Describe area(s) of anger in your life that with God's help you are changing from master to servant.

In addition to Christ, who will you look to for continued accountability for support in dealing with anger?

Selected Bibliography

Augsburger, David, *Caring Enough to Confront.* Glendale: Regal Books, 1980.

Balswick, Jack and Judith, *The Dual-Earner Marriage: The Elaborate Balancing Act.* Grand Rapids: Revell, 1995.

Carlson, Dwight L., *Overcoming Hurts and Anger.* Eugene, Oregon: Harvest House Publishers, 1981.

Carter, Les, and Frank Minirth, *The Anger Workbook.* Nashville: Thomas Nelson Publishers, 1993.

Cosgrove, Mark P., *Counseling for Anger: Resources for Christian Counseling.* Dallas: Word Publishing, 1988.

Dobbins, Richard D., *Your Emotional and Spiritual Power.* Old Tappan, New Jersey: Fleming H. Revell, 1984.

Holland, N. Elizabeth, M.D., *Godly Parenting: Parenting Skills at Each Stage of Growth Group Workbook.* Chattanooga: Turning Point Ministries, 1995.

Jacobs, Joan, *Feelings.* Wheaton: Tyndale House, 1976.

Lee, Jimmy Ray, *Behind Our Sunday Smiles.* Grand Rapids: Baker Book House, 1991.

_____, *Insight Group Workbook, Third Edition.* Chattanooga: Turning Point Ministries, 1995.

Minirth, Frank and Paul Meier, *Happiness Is A Choice.* Grand Rapids: Baker Book House, 1978.

_____, Richard Meier, and Don Hawkins, *The Healthy Christian Life: the Minirth-Meier Clinic Bible Study Guide.* Grand Rapids: Baker Book House, 1988.

Oliver, Gary Jackson and H.Norman Wright, *When Anger His Home.* Chicago: Moody Press, 1992.

Parrott III, Les, *Helping The Struggling Adolescent.* Grand Rapids: Zondervan, 1993.

Schmidt, Jerry and Raymond Brock, *The Emotions of a Man.* Eugene: Harvest House, 1983.

Springle, Pat, *Codependency: A Christian Perspective—Breaking Free from the Hurt and Manipulation of Dysfunctional Relationships.* Houston: Rapha Publishing/Word, 1993.

Wright, H. Norman, *The Power of a Parent's Words.* Ventura, CA: Regal, 1990.

_____, *Communication: Key to Your Marriage.* Glendale: Regal, 1974.

Workbook: *Anger: Our Master or Our Servant*, Turning Point, P. O. Box 22127, Chattanooga, TN 37422-2127

Is there any good reason why you cannot receive Jesus Christ right now?

How to receive Christ:

1. Admit your need (that you are a sinner).

2. Be willing to turn from your sins (repent).

3. Believe that Jesus Christ died for you on the cross and rose from the grave.

4. Through prayer, invite Jesus Christ to come in and control your life through the Holy Spirit (receive Him as Savior and Lord).

What to Pray

Dear God,
I know that I am a sinner and need Your forgiveness.
I believe that Jesus Christ died for my sins.
I am willing to turn from my sins.
I now invite Jesus Christ to come into my heart and life as my personal Savior.
I am willing, by God's strength, to follow and obey Jesus Christ as the Lord of my life.

_____
Date   Signature

The Bible says: "Everyone who calls on the name of the Lord will be saved." *Romans 10:13*

"Yet to all who received Him, to those who believed in His name, He gave the right to become children of God." *John 1:12*

"Therefore, since we have been justified through faith, we have peace with God through our Lord Jesus Christ." *Romans 5:1*

When we receive Christ, we are born into the family of God through the supernatural work of the Holy Spirit who lives within every believer. This process is called regeneration or the new birth.

Share your decision to receive Christ with another person.

Workbook: *Anger: Our Master or Our Servant*, Turning Point, P. O. Box 22127, Chattanooga, TN 37422-2127